SPIROGLYP

Landscape

Tight Spirals, Archemedes Spirals, Hexagon Spirals

BOOK

This Book Belongs To

_____

Spiroglyphics Book

How to Color a Spiroglyphic?

A spiroglyphic consists of two spirals, joined at the middle, that vary in width as they wind towards the centre.

Insert a thin cardboard or a few extra sheets of paper between the pages to avoid ink staining another spiroglypic.

Pick up a pen, preferably a black felt tip pen or sharpie with a thin tip, as some lines are very thin and require more precision.

Start at an outer end of the spiral (it doesn't matter which) and just colour towards the middle. Pause there to see if you can discern what the image is, then work out along the other spiral to the edge again.

Have Fun.

Tight Spirals

The traditional spiroglyphic is the tight spiral. A tight spiral has two starting points, one at the top and the other at the bottom. The user will start at one point and work their way in and, continuing to follow the spiral, will work their way back out again. A suggested starting point has already been included. See the picture below for an example.

start here ↓

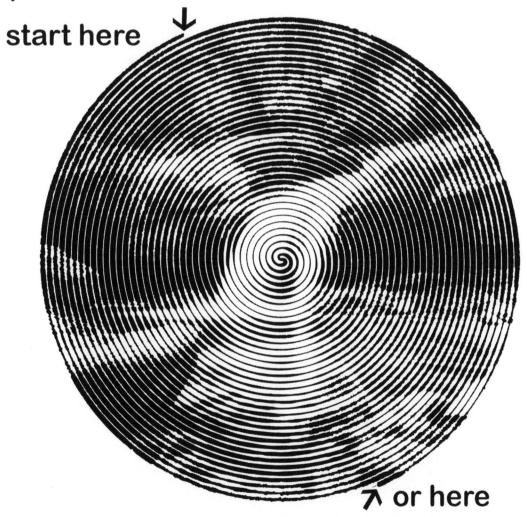

↗ or here

Archemedes Spirals

The Archemedes Spiral is similar to the Tight Spiral. However, unlike the Tight Spiral, it only has one starting point. Start from the outside and work your way in

start here

Hexagon Spirals

The Hexagon Spiral is the most complicated Spiroglyphic, but can be very fun. Unlike its two counterparts, you have to start in the middle and work your way out. In addition, a border also needs to be inked in.

start here

Have Fun!

Have Fun!

Have Fun!

Have Fun!

Have Fun!

Have Fun!

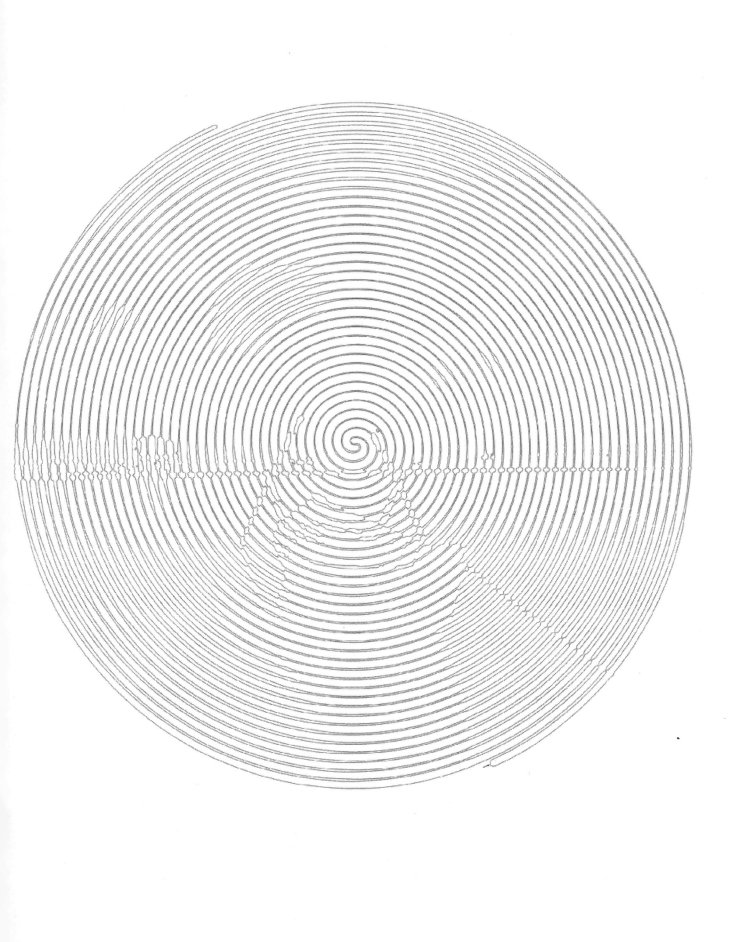

Have Fun!

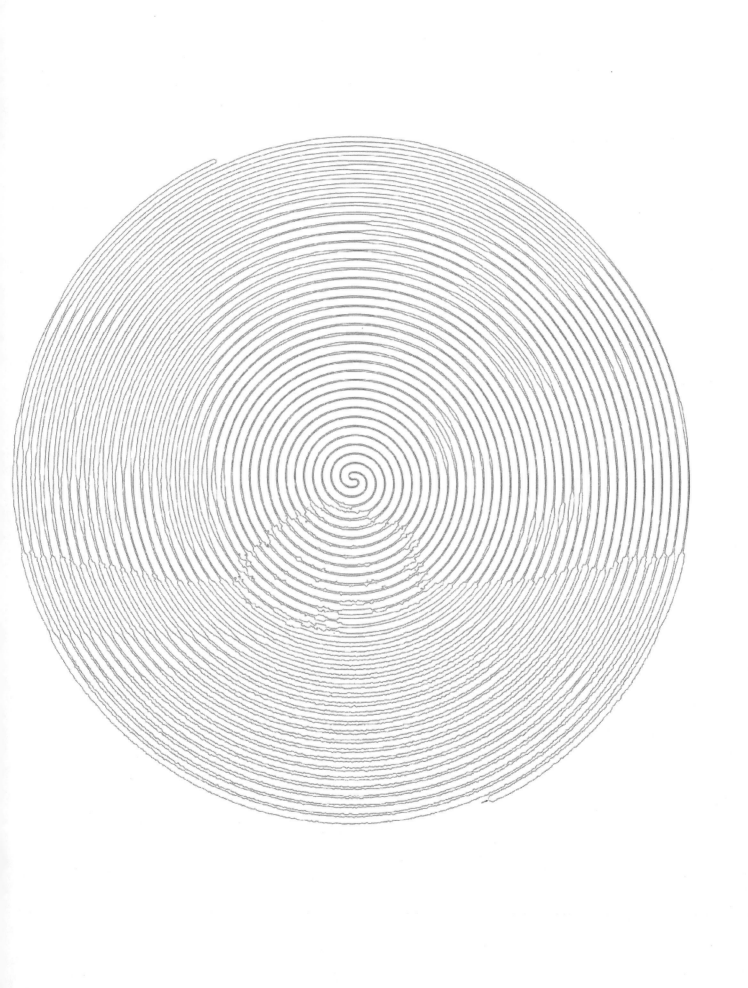

Have Fun!

Have Fun!

Have Fun!

Have Fun!

Have Fun!

Have Fun!

Have Fun!

Have Fun!

Have Fun!

Have Fun!

Have Fun!

Have Fun!

Have Fun!

Have Fun!

Have Fun!

Have Fun!

Have Fun!

Thank You
For
Your Support!

Printed in Great Britain
by Amazon